AT THE WATERS' CLEARING

Nigel McLoughlin

FLAMBARD

The Black Mountain Press

Acknowledgements

Acknowledgement is due to the editors of the following publications, who have published or accepted for publication poems contained in this collection: *Poetry Ireland, Fortnight, Cyphers, Honest Ulsterman, Ropes, Irish Times, Sunday Tribune, Force 10, Books Ireland, The Shop, Black Mountain Review, Electric Acorn, The Big Spoon, The Cork Literary Review, InCognito, Agenda, Acumen, Envoi, The New Writer, Orbis, Outposts, Spondee* (US) and *The Harp* (Japan). Acknowledgement is also due to the following radio stations where some of these poems were first broadcast: Radio Ulster, Radio Foyle and Anna Livia FM.

First published in the UK in 2001 by Flambard Press
Stable Cottage, East Fourstones, Hexham NE47 5DX
and Black Mountain Press
PO Box 9, Ballyclare, Northern Ireland BT39 0JW
Típeset by Haírígh Ó Nuabhaich
Cover design by Keith Connolly, Tonic Design
Additional input by Gainford Design Associates
Author photograph by Declan O'Doherty
Printed in England by Cromwell Press, Trowbridge, Wiltshire

A CIP catalogue record for this book
is available from the British Library.
ISBN 1 873226 50 0
© 2001 Nigel McLoughlin
All rights reserved

Flambard Press wishes to thank Northern Arts
for its financial support.

The publishers wish to thank the Arts Council of Northern Ireland
for financially supporting this publication.

Website: www.flambardpress.co.uk

Contents

In Falcarragh

after Austin Clarke

The wind is soughing at the gable,
Singing to the creeping damp,
Where the moon's cold flag rises
High over Magheraroarty. A pallid
Light bends the tide from Tory
Crossed by a flicker regular as waves.
It's as though the windows breathe

A chill to the cold hearth and I
Weather out each gust, proof
Under blankets to my chin.
Only the occasional star intrudes
Like an eye in the glass pane
And I know this roof will stand
The blast and bar the wind.

I decamp and close the curtains,
Fill the room with a cold dark
Tide, return to snuggle close
To soft skin where her eyes
Smile back at me through black.
I reach for her face and drift and kiss
The mouth beside me and forget.

Missing Her at 4am

In searching for a shadow
(The silhouette of her)
That haunts the hidden
Corners of my mind,
I call it out
And give it substance –
While amid the pallor
Of an ice-blue dawn,
A cold sun
And crimson fingers creep
To burn her image
On an empty bed.

Driven Home

I have framed it
In the mind's quarterlight:
That whitewashed house
The hills backed onto,
A slight increase in light,
Clouds passing, frost
Echoing to the air, words
Across silence, drifting,
Driving the predawn hour home
Across unopened country.

I had come fresh from you,
Unshowered, to the car, still
Tasting you, still heavy with
Your scent. I drove across
Dawn home, as mountains
Unmapped from mist,
From horizon. I pictured
You sleepless in the quiet
Of that house, left to drive
Your lack of dreams
Across unopened country.

On Rosnowlagh Beach

I watched the sunset brush-blush
Her face, and everywhere
The air was darkening. The sky
Still lit, remained a reverse rainbow.
Cyan-sided and shot through
With burnt orange, it flamed through surf.
The sea lapped white noise from
The distance and spread it over sand.
No other sound existed; no other light.

Walking up the beach, we were two
Shadows frozen in the wind, coated,
Gloved and draped in embrace.
We warmed winter with a kiss,
Lit skies with laughter and
Our whispers drowned the sea.

Foreland Heights in the Age of Mechanical Reproduction

for Matt Fluharty

Whiskey glass on the table. Tan on black marble (imitation).

I knew a guy once, drank lighter fuel, lit a cigarette. Immolated from the inside out, over a woman.

Lip sweet the liquid, burning in the throat, the stomach. Can I buy you another?

The woman at the bar is hitching her skirt, enticing me over. She needs a light.

And what if I be with her tonight? Who knows? I find the grinding music of her stimulating somehow. Yes, I could be with her tonight.

My glass is empty. I push it over the bar to the brown-eyed waitress, waiting to be served. I can tell she's in no hurry.

My lips will be wet soon enough. I strike a match and conversation flares between me and the woman to my left. Her skirt is halfway up her thigh. I eye her legs.

I leave with her, the easy swing of her hips in time with mine. Her eyes deceive me closely.

And in the morning we will both wake early, make some excuse to leave.

Three Ways of Looking at It

for Cathal Ó Searcaigh

I am Narcissus in a hall of mirrors.
The walls are lined with pictures,
Reverberating echoes of the dead.

I am the youth in the river.
I smile at those who smile at me.
Narcissus jumped, I shattered.

I am Echo, lover of Narcissus.
I agree with everything he says,
So when he said, 'I'm going to jump!',

'Jump!' I said.

Aisling

Air crept over shadows, silently;
Distilled sunset from the furthest
Shore and sparked it over water,
Lightly, to where you lay sleeping
In my arms.

Sirius shone those August days
When the cooling air became
A climacteric on the skin, weathering
You into me as I drew you close,
Inhaled you.

And you in your dreaming drifted
Across a field of stars and clouds,
Across an expanse of ocean, returned
To touch me as I leaned to kiss you
And you woke.

Subjects

He's keeping time with a pencil
On the page, to the slow air
The fiddler's bowing. Drawing her.

He flicks fine hair across her neck
Shading her cheeks, her hands;
Eyeing her, eyeing her constantly.

He's measuring her, all thumbs.
Angling her with pencils, stopping
Sometimes, proportioning; divining her.

*

There is a feel of 3B about
Her soft graphite eyes.
They never stray, remaining
Fixed to the back wall, lost.

Her hands are dancing, across
The fiddleneck, small hands
Trimmed, with a scrubbed look;
Feline in their fall across strings.

Her face has a high colour
Like an afterglow or blush,
Perhaps from the effort of playing,
Perhaps aware she's being sketched.

The Plan

It's a bartering of dreams,
As they cugger in the snug:
The old man half-sniggering,
Fixing the younger with a wry
Grin and eyes that dance
Behind black frames.

He's brought him out to wet
The baby's head, bought him
Whiskey and water, proffered
A cigarette, called him
Son. And in between
'What are you going to call him?'
And 'What weight did you say?'
He's saying something else:

It's time for you to take
Second place, my son,
Come, stand in my shoes.

Darkling

You could see the old lachico
Any day, perched on the park
Bench, paying out the hours till
Sunset on beads of bread he fed
To birds. He appeared half-*sídhe*
Half-*saoi*, speaking rarely to
Any but the pigeons and the air.

He told me once that he came
Early to the outside of this world,
That he had always known he
Had no share in it. He hid behind
His closed mouth, his fear,
His unransomed loneliness.
One day, he died there.

I went to his wake, one of the few
Willing to associate, who knew
He was harmless, less mad than he
Looked. And kneeling in the dark
Between two candles, I think I found
The word that stiffened on his lips, what
Prayer exhumed from the weeping wax.

*

He had eyes that could be tears
In tallow, could guide him
Through the darkness under
The *lios*, where the night,
He'd tell you, danced like lovers'
Fingers on the skin. It was his:
The entire yielding black element.

It had named him early for its own,
Had mothered him and fathered him,
And warmed him in the comfort of alone.
It lingered on him still, a salt kiss
On those wax lips, as though his words
Might rise and fill the room: Come,
This way friend, feel your way in;
The dark is a woman with soporific skin.

Firesides

i.m. Madeline McLoughlin

Each Halloween she'd sit,
My grandmother, spinning yarns
And teaching the art of divination.

Her chosen medium, hazelnuts,
Licked by flame, drowned in ash,
Would spit and fizzle on the fire.

And in the end they'd burst
As we eyed them, one to the other,
Waiting to find out who'd die first.

She was full of old wives' tales
Of *bean sídhe, madadh mór* and
Coach d'bádhmhar, well versed in portents.

She was at home in these dark days.
And when her shell burst first
I'd catch her smiling, proven right.

At eighty-four she left an empty hearth
Without a sound, no yelping dogs,
No coach wheels, no keening.

Quick, like a shell splitting,
A short hiss of kernel, absolute,
As one who had known all along.

*

And now, I'm sitting here, raking
Over these old coals, at the tail
End of the night. To raise some
Barrier against the February cold
That threatens my bones.

It's now that I remember her,
As I turn the coal-face to the flame,
Stare into embers, draw the sofa
Close and stretch my hands
To the heat, almost catch it.

And as I wring my hands around it,
The mannerism strikes me as hers;
Awakes an old homespun saying:
Even when the coal is burnt,
The embers dead, the ashes cold,

There is something of the fire left.

The Gathering

for Gréagóir Ó Dúill

Finally we'd had enough, downed tools
And sat on kit bags, striking matches,
Firing cigarettes and smoking. We sang
A language of old songs. The sergeants barked
And the air turned blue, but we refused
The polished French of officers, until at last
The colonel asked what it was we wanted.
Let us go home, home to the harvest.

We went in a single wave to the scythe
Of machine-gun fire, the French guns
At our backs. Yards from the German
Lines, mowed row by row, they left us
Where the dark earth gathered in and we
Went home, home to the harvest.

Image

Suited up for Sunday,
Before they took you,
Dressed you in khaki,
And sent you, rifled,
To the Dardanelles.

I got your name, second-hand,
Passed down with details,
Sketches of your life –
Your death in the military
Hospital in Wales.

I know nothing of the dreaming
Years, before the barbed wire,
Bullets and the mines left you
In a regimental plot that
None of us have ever seen.

I could even doubt you,
Put you down as a family
Myth, were it not for this
Photograph, the sole survivor,
I keep as proof –

To imagine what was
Going on behind your
Familiar, familial eyes;
Why, the day you left,
You were smiling.

Breaking Clocks

Beginning each identical grey morning –
The only blue, the bus that passed him by –
His life is beaten out, repeated,
In the seven-second cycle of his machine.
Going through his usual social motions,
Nightly, he oils his throat again,
Down at the local, talking football.
Even that's no longer an escape.

But when he dreams his way above the thicket,
Out past the landfill of his life,
Then the sky unmapping into mountains
Opens up a clearer kind of eye.
Here he can unravel any colour.
He can put the roof upon his half-built life.
He can feel the clocks have all been broken,
Feel the sky rush through the flight of birds.

Urban Myth

It started surreptitiously
To appear, spray-painted,
On fences, walls, flagstones:
MENTOL + GAIL
In black block letters.
It grew more daring,
Running from the sides of trains;
Jumping from the tops of bridges.

Legends started, spread,
Of mad bikers and beautiful
Girls in leather dangling
From the undersides of tunnels.
It was everywhere for a while;
On roundabouts; on the backs
Of busses and, some say, shaved
On a monkey's arse in Belfast Zoo.

I used to wonder if they
Settled down to kids,
A mortgage maybe or
Perhaps a career with
Saatchi or the circus.
Then I saw a skinny
Skinhead spraying on
The wall at Queen's:

MENTOL + GAIL
In black block letters.
I asked if he was Mentol
(Or Gail perhaps)
And he said, 'No, but
My mate is Mentol,
And anyway, Mentol
Would have writ it,
If he'd been here.'

Anti-Sestina

It is not my way to form
Lines with such regularity
As these. Nor keep repeating,
Constantly, the same six
Words in quick succession, to wall
Up a poem, make it wear a mask.

The boundaries my emotions mask
Cannot be framed within a form
Dictated by a solid wall
Constructed brick by brick with regularity
Relying on these same six
To shore it up, repeating

Forever repeating,
Like layer upon layer of masks
Lying one upon the other six
Deep to form
With aching regularity –
A wall.

Or even a series of such walls,
Even worse, concentric circles, repeating
Steady as a metronome, regularity –
Bland as masks;
No change, no way to form
A vigorous complexity. Just six

Nails in a coffin, holding a dead poem six
Stanzas long. If I could I'd outlaw walls,
Play a little with the form,
Stop all the endless repeating,
Drag off the mask,
Force it to beautiful ir-regularity.

But they won't let me do away with regularity
Those who favour using only six
Words to make a masque
Of art, of life, who love wall-
-ing in explosions of emotion, love repeating
All the same old forms.

So once again, with regularity, I say: Tear down the wall!
Forget the six fixed words, forget repeating.
A masque-rade is never true to form.

Some Go Dancing

'Some who go dancing through dark bogs are lost'
                    (Louis MacNeice)

There could be emeralds,
Topaz, amethysts in the sky
Where the setting sun
Makes a tiger's eye
Of the horizon.

The light sublimes
Under night's arced wing
Like a jewelled shock
Of hair that springs
From mountains.

It's nights like these she comes,
A fickle witch, her red hair down,
Drawing me to the hills
That lie outside the town,
And takes me dancing.

And I have danced with her
Where the moon sings
Impaled in branches, or drowns
In streams that dragon wing
The hillsides.

And there are nights she leaves
Me to find my own way home
And I have danced down mountains,
Through dark bogs, have never known
That I was lost.

Cat at My Window

A black cat with cyan eyes
Watches me from my window.
A buckle-back arches hair
To heaven and a pink slit
Is bitten out from teeth.
The face is feminine,
Too small to be intimidating.
Yet she looms at my window.

A shadow on the night,
The borders of her body blur,
Melt into the outside, indistinctly
Until she becomes as massive
As sky. The cyan eyes, lights
In the huge beast of night.
Her soundless mouthings under
Glass, lost cries at her changing.

Lines

for James McLoughlin

I

The lines were run in circles
Into boxes, measured out in yards,
Checking each hook and spanning
Breastbone to fist for the next,
Cursing the barb-bite of a stray.

The lines were lifted early, set late.
The time between, a fury of mending,
Checking, baiting, and driving drums
To the Dutchman to be weighed. Lunch
Was eels, fried still moving on the pan.

II

Lines of eels thrown lithe-live
Into an old oil drum in my uncle's boat.
Once, I tossed the drum, fell,
Screamed under their oozing mass
And always after fished for pike.

III

The little ones I carried home
Forefinger and thumb in either eye,
Larger ones were middle-finger
Gaffed under the last gill, taken
To be gutted, skinned and fried.

Jawbones of the biggest, boiled
And bleached, I kept for trophies.
With my fingers slashed by gills
Of one only stunned, I spent my summers
Dodging bailiffs and water-rats.

IV

Each assassin tempted out of reed-clumps
With live bait. Sink and draw, drawing out
The fight to complete capitulation on lines
Without trace-wire. My landing net was
A cold wet slapping on concrete piers.

V

Of the men who fished Lough Erne
Professionally, few could swim
And none would fish at Whit.
It is said the lough takes three
Lives every year, in memory

Of a sacrifice to the old god
Who lives two miles from shore
In the pit of the Broad Lough,
Where light stops and weights
Have failed to hit the bottom.

Even I, who stood on piers,
Threw lines where I would not go,
Pulled pike for fear of eels,
Even I stayed well away at Whit
Out of respect, fearing a slip.

VI

I've seen an eel cross land,
Snake its way to water with
A muscular will to live. Even
With the head cut off they thrash
For hours, and if you poke a finger
Into the headless gullet, you can feel
The suck as it pulls towards the stomach.

VII

It's a peaceful death, they say,
But that's a lie that fishermen tell
To comfort relatives of the bloated
Corpse they drag, mangled, from lough
Gates or the net's mesh, mouths wide

In a watered scream, hands full
Of grass and weed they gripped so tight
The fingers must be broken to release it.
They say, you drown by thirds, three chances
To be caught and dragged thrashing back

To land, gulping air and fighting
For your life. Three breaths before
Water sucks your dream and thought
Dissolves, before everything is water,
Your eye wide and cold as the pike's.

VIII

I learned to swim
When I stopped fishing,
Left my singing reel,
Left my line to rot.

The only thing I could not
Leave, the lough, the water,
Called me back as a mother
Would a straying child.

I never left it long. There
Is a bond of blood that pulls
Me to it: several ancestors
Dead by drowning.

IX

These days I run my lines by metre
Not the yard, but still I circle,
Box them in and check the hooks.
I run them shore to shore, have pushed
Apart the weight, the float and set
My lines to fish the deeper water.

Earthed

Just a foretaste of storm to come:
Winter in juvenilia, playing, testing,
Its strength, or the strength of walls.
The wind gives voice to gables
And trees are singing, soon
I think, it will tear down the eaves.
The rain is a burglar, stealing in
Through the window seal and
The glass is melting, slowly.

But I have seen the storm full-grown
Lay trees across roads like ladder rungs,
Leave wires sparking in the sheugh.
I have felt it bellow me backwards, drive
Me to the fireside, instinctively, when
The sky lit jaggedly, and thunder tore.
I have watched my mother run to cover
Mirrors, draw curtains across windows,
Remove the tongs, render the hearth safe.

So what is this? A tantrum, a child's mewling?
My fear has been outgrown, cast off, I find
Logic better fitted. Electricity seeks ground
Not glass. I don't believe these old wives'
Tales of lightning bullets that ricochet.
Still, I won't stand at windows
To watch lightning, to face down the fury,
For even though I'm not the tallest standing
Arrows miss their mark; accidents happen.

Storm Front

Nights like these are separable:
There is a certain music to them;
To that wind's weird whistle
Through wires, rising and falling,
Breathing almost.
The pizzicato rain falling in strings
Is unrelenting, precipitating

The otherworldly from the dip
In temperature to that electricity;
That tingling in the teeth.
It's a something other than sound
That keeps me awake, alert, waiting.
Nights like these are portentous:
There is a sense of happenings.

Nights like these are for the divining
Of omens from the air and the knocking
Of distant doors; receiving news.
A new moon laments the dividing sky;
A lullaby, the slow turning of the clock.

These are nights for huddled stories,
Where fire first sprang from flint;
Nights of creeping silence;
Listening in the dark;
Waiting for the breaking of the storm;
Waiting for the light.

Nights like these are umbilical:
The past courses to the present
And it is close.

Songs for the Years' Turning

I Imbolc

Knitting words into silence,
Incanting at the hearthstone,
Where fire lights the hag's eyes,
Blind, she's remembering:
Each noviciate gathering rushes
By the shore's edge;
Each woman weaving crooked crosses;
The low moans around gables;
Every *bean sídhe*.
She's remembering
All the things she's been
And keening for the years' turning.

II Beltaine

The snowdrop pushes soil,
Screams out rebirth,
As juices ooze upward in
A slow sexing under eaves.
Under the bark, fused
To the explosion, the bursting
Of the buds is almost audible.
Take all of this, each landing
And leaving time, and dedicate
It to the god of death, of change.
For with each dive and circle, birds
Are flinging to the sun
Their songs for the years' turning.

III Lughnasa

The journey is a short one
From a borrowed throne
To the sage's seat.
And for a master of all the arts
There is only dissolution left,
Sweating groundward.
The air reeks of elder and heat,
Where the old dogs are lying,
Fleas cracking, in the sun;
And each movement labours
Like slow music
At the year's turning.

IV Samhain

The mind aquaplanes
Into mist, free falls
To omens, portents, ghosts.
These are the dark days,
Blurred borders.
That first wind that cuts
The sallies, names it:
Night of the world's dreaming.
The hooded crows are cloaking
Their black secrets from the moon
And forgotten gods are gathering
Around fires in the hills, where
The Morrigan is dancing
To the song of each year's turning.

Two Songs

after John Berryman

Among the stone and rock
Of my bleak garden grew
A fragile bluebell, singular,
Mr Bones, and true
To its colour, being frocked
Everywhere by gravel; its head angular.

Until the day that Henry sent
The box by post, huge
And wooden and rectangular,
Edges sharp with letters rouged
'This way up', it meant
To keep the contents straight, untangled.

The postman left it on the ground
Just outside the door, pushed
Up against the wall.
I found the fragile bluebell crushed
And stencilled black: 'Breakable'. I found
Nothing inside it, nothing at all.

*

I took to the drink after that.
You can't imagine the effect
That alcohol has, Mr Bones,
Brings a focus I never knew I had, deflects
Perspective from the pat
And turns the senses, turns the mind to stone.

* – I know it, man, I know it.*
*   I've seen what it can do.*
*   I've been there oftentimes myself,*
*   Man, I wish I was you.*
Well, Mr Bones, I grow
Wearier each day. I worry about my health.

What do you do when life has lost its fun?
* – I don't know, maybe sit down and talk*
*   Or fetch another bottle from the fridge.*
Mr Bones I think I'll take a walk.
* – Where you goin', son?*
I'm going to the bridge.

The Yellow Bittern

from the Irish of Cathal Buí Mac Giolla Ghunna

I grieve, yellow bittern, over your death;
The sorry stretching of your bones.
For it was not hunger but the drouth
That left you lying belly-up and dead.
Far worse, this fate, than any fall of Troy,
To die upon the coul' bare stones.
You did no harm to any but yourself.
You drank ditchwater as well as any wine.

Beautiful bittern, my distress is great
To see you flat out upon the road.
Each day I would hear your boom astride
Your midden, gargling as you drank.
Many think your brother, Cathal, will meet
The selfsame end as you, not true,
My handsome bird, I know they're wrong
For it was want of drink that killed your song.

Young bittern, ah my sorrow's huge,
To see you stuck among the reeds,
The big rats traipsing to your wake
To have their fun and eat their fill.
If only you'd sent news in time
Of your need of drink, your sorry bind.
I'd have broken a hole in Vesey's lake,
To wet your lips and grease your throat.

I'll make no laments for other birds,
Not corncrake, cuckoo or grey heron,
But you my yellow bittern, full of heart,
Were my own like in style and colour.
I knew well you loved your drink,
And many say that I'm the same,
But I'll drink all I can rap and run,
For fear I die of thirst like you.

My girl says I should quit the drink
Or I'll not live much longer. But I
Told her to houl' her whist for
Drinking makes me all the stronger.
Did you not all see that smooth-necked bird,
Dead in a ditch, a short time back?
Well pals, put the bottle clean to your heads,
And take a drop to ease you; for you're a long time dead.

The Green Man

from the Irish of Cathal Ó Searcaigh

You ride in from the outback on the back of the wind,
Loose-limbed, hob-nailing a storm. I smell whin, fresh
On the gale of your breath. The ooze of the bog drips the green
Sod of your tongue and flocks of birds sing like leaves in
Your hair's cowl. You come inciting seed, the roots' fingering
And bidding sun's lustre to the grey face of April.

The clouds are tangling in your limbs and birds nest
In your chest's heather, settle in the hedgerow of your loins.
Yet you come scouring, pelting the cuckoo out with rain
That drives a sheen on weed and bush and blackthorn.
And when you stretch the spring of your bones
There is a bleat in the field and a crake in the meadow.

Here, in this mountain pasture, the green light of your eye
Dives into our clay and hope is full in bud and feather.

Restoration

Lightning. Rain crashing on the window pane, to wake me
and keep me writing. I'm drawn to storms, to the darkness of
the tree that looms across the lake.

You can still see the scars on the trunk where the car hit,
they've grown over now, faint reminders of deeper cuts in the
soft pith of parents and friends.

The night after the car wreck I walked the road beyond the
tree at two or three o'clock in the morning. Winter, with my
crombie coat tucked about my chin, head down into the wind
and rain. I pushed myself home.

Nights later, I passed a poppy wreath blowing between road
and ditch, thinking it would not be found come morning. But
returning home just after dawn, I saw it thrown back beneath
the tree. A chance act of the last gust.

Kilmakerrill

Halfway between Manorhamilton and Glenfarne,
There is a place just off the road
Whose name rings out with loneliness.
Kilmakerrill – a burial ground,
Where graves are cut from granite soil,
And the stone is rough.
A thousand years of bone and rock
(And maybe a thousand more)
Lie in that uneven ground.

This is the place where generations
Of my ancestors rest,
Lying line upon line
In close-knit family groups.
Here within the rough rock wall
The gravestones grow
Out of the very earth
Like dragons' teeth.

On this open plain,
Lashed by winds
That shake the soul –
There bleeds true freedom;
And all who lie within know
The cruelty of true peace.
Bury me here, when my time
Above the sod is over.

There is no church
To stand over it,
No church for miles around
But here all rest –
And no God gazes down.

Unearthly, silent at night,
So silent that you can hear
The grass whisper:

Here a man can be truly dead,
And a corpse completely cold.

Funeral

The accelerating years plunge
From birth to earth like
The short trajection of a hurtling bird.

The frightening ground approaches,
Sudden as a bullet, impact or
The stopping of a quickening clock.

Those eyes on me, as
My tear-dried throat
Stumbles over *Avés*.

Aware of the gaping grave,
Its need for filling in,
I hold what little ground I have.

Later at your grave, I unroll
Words like a carpet, even
And unafraid, warming

My communion, alone and in the dark.

The Gift

i.m. John Tummon

Smiling secretly to yourself somewhere
Between the purse of a slow air and the belt
Of a reel as though you know that you
And not the wood are the true instrument,
That music is merely sparks in the head
Forced to look for a lightning rod.

At the point where the tune took off
You'd close your eyes and disappear
Into a state of grace where sparks flew
And fire spat through wood. You'd wring
Tears from timber, turning and turning
The tune through the furrows of your head.

That is how I'll always picture you:
In a maze of melody, notes like flames
Around your head and your eyes closed,
At once lost and unified with music, fingers
Raised to dance the air in the semi-dark.
I wish you peace and a state of grace,

Here, this long night, I offer this:
A rod for grief's cold lightning.

Crossings

i.m. Damian Quinn

I'm sure I saw a fug of fox
High-tail to the dark and green-
Eyed ditch under the fog and out
Of the corner of an eye. The road
Bent and the lights caught the lake
On the fall and a fish split
The surface for a second in
A small shingle of light where

The cold eye of the lake stared
Through a lens of frost and fixed
The colour-blind moon in focus.
Trees groaned under the weight
Of black air that draped on
The rumpled sheet of land and hills
Crowding back to back in coats
And shawls as though the world
Was nothing but a lake of shadows.

The morning brought a white rime
And a dagger wind that cut me blue
Where I stood as they put you down.
The rosary ebbed and flowed and finally
Abated and I drove the same road home
In daylight. The world was nothing
But a lake of mist and shadow yet
I'm sure I saw that same fox high-
Tail to the ditch and turn red-eyed
To face me at the waters' clearing.

Borders

I can feel all the borders
Merge here, as silence bends
Under a burden of sound yet
Remains unbroken somehow.
The dark drives into light
Without driving it away;
Water marries land in the bog
And sky meets mountain in the mist;
These roads and fields grow
Into eachother intimately.

From here I feel no need
To look skyward; I can see
Clouds creep as shadows
Overland, watch a mist of rain
Drift westward and die out.
Distinction is a small thing
Here, a drift from sleep
To waking, a breathing
And unbreathing, listening
To a yellow bird, his
Intermittent speaking,
A disembodied voice.

Diminuendo

The thickening air of evening comes
Dripping from eaves, empurples
Daylight, roosts in trees.

The birds protest the dusking sun;
Dirge the descending density of dark,
Their song dropping cadence to the wind.

Here dwell the silences, ghosting
Reflections to the silhouette of sound,
Mirroring the calends of a longer night.

Just a Shade

Just a shade darker, this water,
Than the colour of her eyes.
Just a shade more silent, this darkness,
Than the silence in her soul.
Just a shade more peaceful, this hillside,
Than the whisperings at twilight
After her words are gone.

Just a shade colder, this night,
Than the cool of her caress.
Just a shade more rhythmic, the surf,
Than the beating of her heart.
Just a shade more still, I,
Standing mute on the hillside, than she,
Just a shade, standing mute on the pier.

Deora Dé

for my mother

'See them?' she said,
And pointed to a yellow
Flower blotched with red,
'They grew below Christ's cross.
And see…' she said, pointing
To each stain, 'the seven
Drops of blood.'

'See them?' she said,
Pointing to the unopened
Fuchsia earrings in the hedge.
She lifted one and nipped
And broke it where the flower
Meets the pod and prising the top
End, 'taste!' she said.

A single drop
Of nectar fell on the end
Of my tongue, surprising
Me with sweetness.
'When God cries,' she said
'His tears are sweet
And red.'

Reaching for the opened version
I did the same.
'See them?' I said,
'Them's little ballerinas,
Red skirts, red tights
And little purple knickers.'
I giggled, twisting

Each dancer to a whirl
In breeze, into a turn
And turn on a green
Backdrop – six pleated
Blurs on the stage
Of a wall.

'You'll never make a priest,'
Was all she said.

Overgrown

Again, I walk these woods;
The forests of my dreams;
Along paths beaten
Flat by children's feet.
I, and others, who ran
And jumped untroubled,
By rivuleted ditches
And brier bushes that hung
Too high to crown us.
The scratches, after all,
Were only skin deep;
The beauty lay deeper,
Well guarded; still untouched.

The thorns are lower now,
Sticking hard and deep
And the ditches are too wide
For any man to jump –
Without fear of drowning.
And so I pick my way,
Precariously, among the roots
Of trees and dreams,
Unscaled now,
But well climbed then,
When I had no fear of falling.

Catching Fire

for Joan and Kate Newmann

She maintained only one right way
To clean the flue: fire shoved
Up to burn it out, drive sparks
From the chimney stack and smuts
Into air. Each bunched and bundled
Paper held till the flame took
And it flew, took off on its own
Consumption, rose on its own updraft.
I stood fixed by her leather face
Dancing in firelight, her hands

Clamped to the metal tongs. Her old
Eyes stared black and wide, rims
Of blue that circled wells, pools
That fire stared into. I watched
Her pull from beneath them black
Ash and a paper smell I love still.
She told me she saw faces in the flame
And people, places, things take place.
She'd spey fortunes there. Told me
Mine. But I saw nothing more or less

Than the dance of flame, the leap
And die, the resurrection of yellow
Cowl and dual change of split-
Levelled flame that held within it
A dance of words, a ballet of images.
I heard only the music of burning,
A soundless consummation of persistence,
Imagined a vision of my hands reddening
Where I stood, felt my knuckles braising,
My bones in tongues, flaming.

Shaking the Moon

for Menna Elfyn

A parabola on a tarzan swing,
A pendulum on the jibbet branch
Of an ossified tree, he creaks his
Way over water.

I envy him his unfear of heights,
His hollered freedom, thrown
To silence as he flings himself,
Aiming for the moon.

I remember the fraying, snapping sound
Like a breaking bone, the slow motion
Ascent, the graceless limb-tangled
Splash landing.

He dragged himself dripping from the lake,
Managed a smile. 'Are you OK?' I asked.
'I think I shook the moon!' he said and
Dropped.

Periodic Table

Magnesium, calcium, sodium, potassium…
Learning by rote the reaction series
Bottom to top, bubble to explosion,

We drudged our way through elements,
The weight, the properties, the reactions,
Compounding the invisible in molecules of water.

I saw soft, chewing-gum metals, sliced and dropped:
The fire, fume and fizzle wished weird
Creatures from dead metal, strange as dragons

In our heads, they lay on our tongues like stones.
Buried cerebellum deep in each, imagination atrophied,
Lurked sulking for the bell. The ringing

Summoned our bravado, lies and nonsense,
Sent them oozing from the hollows, like metals
Pulled from electrolyte, set them dancing

Like Kekulé's monkeys around our heads.

Quarterlights

1 View from the Garden

It's just a short walk from mist
Into the dark. A statue's head peeps
Over a low wall to frighten lovers.
Telegraph poles stand like gibbets
And birds whistle nervously in the dark.

In the mist each moonbeam lights
The trees, vernal with verdigris. A garden
Of remembrance, never planted; a grown-
Over bomb site; a half-demolished
Building; a monument covered up.

The car park's chasm is overrun
With *Beetles* and trees haloed by the moon
Stand silent as unknown soldiers, on guard.
The only sound remains my feet
And the echoes in the silent places.

2 View from the Town

A street of palaces and pubs;
A courthouse crumbling and the church.
Hairdressers, whorehouses, leaded windows,
Lattices and lechers, levity and debt.
This is Ireland.

Artificial arches, wallpaper and weeping;
Defunct post-office, townhall, death.
Chemists, chandeliers; litterbins and layabouts;
Dolls' houses, dole offices, marriage, drink.
Buttresses and old banks, bridal boutiques
Shutters down against the cold.

Toyshops and graveyards, taxis and takeaways,
Hardware, software, charities and change.
Bank machines and bridges; bread and breakdowns;
Jewellers, general stores, butchers and tourists;
One bookshop, one town centre, all ivy and atrophy,
And in the middle of it – mist.

3 View from the Hill

Sky blue-black near dawn
And mist pervading pockets
Of full-moon light.
The town lights, pale red
And yellow, pin-pricks of sadness
On the mirror of the lough.

Translucent hues, skeletal trees;
Orange and white bouncing
From the upper veils
Of valleys filled like cups,
Under breasted hills and paths
Where in the daylight years
We courted – just sixteen.

I can taste the air
Light as star-glow
Sharp and rich; clear.
I stand breathing life in;
Soul out like mist.

4 View from the Lough

Standing on a bridge, below a graveyard,
One step away from being entombed
In mist lying six feet deep, over water.
Where eerie silence and full moon glare
Light candles of recognition
In a lover's lonely stare.

Asking name of name – two lovers
Stand twisted, clasping hands –
Exchanging. Two beech saplings,
In mutual support, leaning inward
Against a brace of black-topped buildings
Brightened by the moon – and moisture.

Reeds rustle over silent lakes;
I sit at a table damp with dew,
Topped with beer cans, lit
By the moon's corona, all hues
And glows and mildew. I strain
My sight to see ten yards ahead.

5 View from the Nightclub

Car radios beat steady as hearts:
Rhythm regulating engines.
Headlights under mist beam yellow
Under paler yellow streetlights;
Dogs bark as a jaundiced sun is rising.

Existing only in shades of carlight laser,
Distant shouts as the nightclub
Throws out its last hoard of drunks.
Lighted cigarettes, flamed imaginations,
And an ambulance swells cold against the night.
A bird sings to the light of the KFC.

Dubhghall

from the Irish of Gréagóir Ó Dúill

All I wanted was a haven.
I'd had enough of wave and tiller,
Of sail billowed by the howling
Whore of a wind on the Irish Sea.

All I wanted was a harbour.
I dragged my ploughshare snout,
My sea-horse neck with a rope of hemp.
I made a camp of my ship, built a fire,
Formed a palisade of oars.
They blossomed.

The oars are standing yet
Among the crimped hair underfoot.
From the corner of my eye, on a far skerry,
I see a cormorant stretch its wings,
My left hand readies my shield
For there is a bonfire on the far hill
And a line of firebrands approaching.
The battle-frenzy is over, my berserks lie stripped,
And the wounds on their backs have dried.

It is my people's custom to torch the ship,
Set it out to sea, the chief's body
Laid out for glory.
It's a ceremony one man can't perform.
Here they come. I start to sing my Valhalla song.

Waiting to become a blood eagle.

Caha

You could crack a match
On the rock inside these tunnels
When they were first chiselled.
Years, it took, with sledgehammers,
Bits and wedges, drilling through
The years before Nobel.

Moveable forges kept the metal true,
Roasted spuds, once daily,
Halfway between dawn and dusk.
A navvy army hammered away daylight,
Fought blow by blow through mountains,
Heard hammers even as they slept.

And after chipping away at time itself,
Choking out summers in the dust,
Battering away winters at the forge,
It must have been like birth
To strike that final blow that let
The air come dancing through the gap.

Belfast

The stroke of a clock on the still air
And the tolling of a bell over water.
These are simple, lonely sounds,
The sounds of a city sleeping.
And each dark silence concentrates
The shape-shifting shadows on the moon.
Consecrates the night; consummates
The concrete's love of moonlight.

A slow dawn mist falls from the Cavehill,
Softly eddies through streets, curls
Around houses, makes myths of murals,
Settles beneath flags.
And this is a city of many flags,
But today it will wake
To its only common colour.

The slow Lagan weaves below
Like a murky dream, black beneath
And white above, it mingles all
Our necessary shades of grey.
The river mist is rolling, birthing
A familiar landscape in something
Less than stone, something more
Than air. It is our dreams almost
Forming, hesitant as a sleeper waking.

63

Stones

Passing Milltown on the last bus home,
The gravestones flicker-flame,
Flare into life, just for seconds,
As if to say...

Remember how we buried truth
Under martyrs, under blame;
When God was which and who,
How we poured blood for pronouns.

The lights of The Maze play in lines,
Dancing chains around the gaol.
Our dead rhetoric returns,
In sentences, parsed with guns.
It echoes off walls...

Haunting our silences, in these places
Where those we've shut up, put
Under stones, form monuments
In years, in tears, in flesh
Bagged by the hundredweight.